A TREASURY OF
HALLOWEEN HUMOR

2022

Happy Hallow-Weenie to Teddy, my pun pal

A TREASURY OF HALLOWEEN HUMOR

Richard Lederer

RICHARD LEDERER

INTERNATIONAL PUNSTER OF THE YEAR

ILLUSTRATED BY JIM MCLEAN

Waterside Productions

Printed in the United States of America

First Printing, 2020

ISBN-13: 978-1-949001-25-9 print edition
ISBN-13: 978-1-949001-26-6 ebook edition

Waterside Productions

2055 Oxford Ave
Cardiff, CA 92007
www.waterside.com

to Doug Haise and Tracy Balistreri,
the very spirits of Halloween

TABLE OF CONTENTS

THE STORY OF HALLOWEEN

Halloween is the year's spookiest holiday. On October 31, we carve glowering faces on pumpkins, put on scary costumes, take our children trick-or-treating, and devour mouth-watering, calorie-laden goodies, which always go to waist.

Only on Halloween do parents encourage their kids to trespass on someone's property, make a non-negotiable demand, and take candy from strangers. One quarter of all the candy sold annually in the United States is purchased for Halloween. Chocolate, which in itself is a major food group, is by far the most popular confection, followed by candy corn.

Americans fork out nine billion dollars, second only to Christmas in consumer spending. One indication of that spending is that twenty percent of American dog owners buy costumes for their pets. In fact, I have a friend who dressed up his dog as a cat for Halloween. Now my friend can't get his dog to come when he calls her.

One of our oldest holidays, Halloween finds its roots in ancient Ireland in the fifth century BCE. The observance signaled the end of the Celtic year and the beginning of the dark, cold winter. The Celts were farmers who worshipped nature. On this day, they observed Samhain, a festival that celebrated the final harvest and the storing of food for the winter ahead. People lit huge bonfires and donned costumes to ward off ghosts.

In time, the Roman Empire conquered the Celts and took over some of their beliefs as well. This included Samhain, which the Romans combined with their own festivals.

Over the centuries, the holiday evolved from its pagan Irish origins, but the people did not forget the early customs. In the eighth century CE, Pope Gregory III introduced All Saints' Day to replace the older festivals honoring the dead. The holiday, celebrated on November 1, was also known as All Hallows' Day, a hallow being a saint or holy person. The preceding night was named All Hallows' Eve, which has been shortened to Hallowe'en, and then to Halloween.

In the second half of the nineteenth century, America was flooded with new immigrants, "huddled masses yearning to breathe free." These fresh arrivals, especially the millions fleeing the Irish potato famine, helped popularize the celebration of Halloween nationally.

In 1920, Anoka, Minnesota, celebrated the first city-wide Halloween with a costumed parade followed by treats for the revelers. The celebration was innovated by several civic organizations in an effort to divert the local youth from Halloween pranks, such as turning cows loose, soaping windows, and toppling outhouses. After that, it didn't take long for Halloween to go nationwide. New York started observing Halloween in 1923 and Los Angeles in 1925.

A FEAST OF HALLOWEEN GOODIES

You may well have heard the seasonal prey upon words "What do you call an empty hot dog?" Answer: *A hollow weenie.* But you may not have realized how expansive is the tricky treat bag of Halloween puns. There's something about the lore of Halloween that inspires tour de farces at the highest level of punnery. The holiday is a veritable Bill of Frights.

Here's a menu that I've cooked up for Halloween. I know you won't be able to resist goblin up this six-corpse meal.

GRAINS

Ghost Toasties   Scream of Wheat
Rice Creepies   Brain Muffins
Pentagram Crackers with Poisonberry Jam

ENTREES

Baby Bat Ribs   Hungarian Ghoul Ash
Fangfurters   Frank 'n' Stein

Deviled Ham   Fillet of Soul
Blood Pudding   Black Catfish
Hag-gis   Hellibut
     Stake Sandwitch with Grave-y
Warlocks and Bagels with Scream Cheese

SIDE DISHES

Artery-Chokes   Strangled Eggs
Deviled Eggs   Gashed Potatoes
Scarrots   Skullions
Pickled Bats   Ghost Liver Pate

Asparagross   Spookghetti
Gangreens   Baked Beings
    Terror-Fried Green Tomatoes

FRUITS

Adam's Apples   Blood Oranges   Necktarines

DESSERTS

I Scream	Lemoan Pie
Booberry Pie	Boo Meringue
Terror-misu	Lady's Fingers
Ghoulda Cheese	Monster Cheese
Creep Suzette	Devil's Food Cake

Haunted Toll House Cookies

Screech Pie topped with Ghoul Whip

BEVERAGES

Ghoul Ade	Coffin with Scream
Demonade	Anxie-tea
Finger Ale	Monster
Zombie	Apple Spider
Cold Bier	Bloody Mary
Blood Light	Witch Hazelnut Coffee
Boos	Tequila Mockingbird

A PUMPKIN PATCH

The Irish tell a story about a notorious drunkard and trickster named Jack. He couldn't enter heaven because he was a miser, and he was unable to enter Hell because he had played practical jokes on the Devil. The Devil gave him a single ember to light his way through the darkness. Jack placed the hot coal inside a hollowed-out turnip to keep it glowing longer and was left to walk the earth until Judgment Day with his "Jack's lantern."

In Ireland grew up the custom of carving out the insides of turnips and filling them with embers to represent the souls of the dead. Irish immigrants brought the tradition to America. Here, they replaced turnips with the more abundant pumpkins to create jack-o'-lanterns, and the practice spread.

Oh my gourd! Let's carve out some humor with a pumpkin patch of riddles. Orange you pumped for this?

What vegetable do you get when you drop a pumpkin?
Squash.

Why did Cinderella suck at softball?
Because her coach was a pumpkin.

What's the favorite food of mathematicians?
Pumpkin pi.

How can you make a jack-o'-lantern stop smoking?
Make him wear a pumpkin patch.

What do you call a jack-o'-lantern living on a farm?
A country pumpkin.

Who helps the little pumpkins cross the road safely?
The crossing gourd.

What do you call a fat jack-o'-lantern?
A plumpkin.

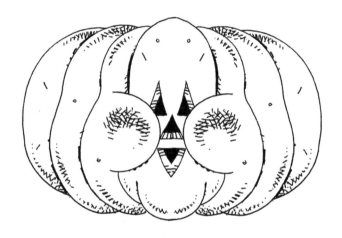

What did the pumpkin say to the pumpkin carver?
"Cut it out!"

What do you call an athletic pumpkin?
A jock-o'-lantern.

How do predatory canines find their way around at night?
They carry jackal lanterns.

How did Mr. Hyde celebrate Halloween?
With a Jekyll lantern.

In honor of the seasonal pumpkin, let's celebrate some words that have one thing in common. They all end with the letters *k-i-n*. Provide the missing letters for each word defined:

1. jack-o'-lantern material   _ _ _ _kin
2. small fellow along the Yellow
   Brick Road   _ _ _ _ _kin
3. lip wiper   _ _ _kin
4. model of the human body   _ _ _ _kin
5. similar   _kin
6. awkward country fellow   _ _ _ _kin
7. NFL ball   _ _ _ _kin

Now step up to some much rarer words that end in *k-i-n*:

8. smooth twill suiting fabric   _ _ _ _ _ _kin
9. hip-length sleeveless jacket   _ _kin
10. dagger or blunt needle   _ _kin
11. knee-high, laced boot   _ _ _kin
12. small wooden vessel or cask   _ _kin
13. spike of tightly clustered
    flowers   _ _kin
14. individual baking dish   _ _ _kin
15. earthenware pot   _ _kin

Using the definitions as clues, identify the following words that begin with the letters *k-i-n:*

16. considerate   kin_
17. monarch   kin_
18. class for children   kin_ _ _ _ _ _ _ _
19. light a fire   kin_ _ _
20. tight curl   kin_
21. far out, eccentric   kin_ _
22. relating to movement   kin_ _ _ _
23. study of movement   kin_ _ _ _ _ _ _
24. archaic plural of *cow*   kin_
25. early TV recording   kin_ _ _ _ _ _

ANSWERS

1. pumpkin 2. Munchkin 3. napkin 4. manikin
5. akin 6. bumpkin 7. pigskin 8. sharkskin 9. jerkin
10. bodkin 11. buskin 12. firkin 13. catkin 14. ramekin 15. pipkin

16. kind 17. king 18. kindergarten 19. kindle
20. kink 21. kinky 22. kinetic 23. kinesiology 24. kine
25. kinescope

BAT TO VERSE

Wthat would you do if you opened your front
door and saw Dracula, Frankenstein's monster, a ghost, a ghoul, King-Kong, a mummy,
Quasimodo, a skeleton, a werewolf, a witch, and a
zombie standing on your steps?

Hope it's Halloween.

Halloween is a time when we conjure up visions
of all manner of ghoulies and ghosties and long-
leggety beasties. We human beings are fascinated by
monsters. We are somehow drawn to their ugliness.
Monsters are ghastly, grotesque, gruesome, hair-
raising, hideous, horrifying, and downright yucky
creatures. They're so ugly that their own shadows
run away from them. They're so ugly that when they
look in a mirror, their reflections look back and
scream. And they're so ugly that when they appear
in *Star Wars* movies, they don't wear costumes.

What is a monster's normal eyesight?
20/ 20/ 20/ 20.

How does a monster count to 25?
On her fingers.

How does a monster count to 50?
On her toes.

Is it okay for a monster to eat fried chicken with her fingers?
No, the fingers should be eaten separately.

Who won the beauty contest for monsters?
Nobody.

What's the difference between a lame sailor and a monster?
One's a gob hobblin' and the other's a hobgoblin.

Why don't monsters remember anything you tell them?
Because what you say will go in one ear and out the others.

FIRST MONSTER MOTHER: "You have the ugliest baby I have ever seen!"
SECOND MONSTER MOTHER: "Thank you very much!"

We humans enjoy the wonderful variety of monsters. The morgue the merrier!

The Headless Horseman laughed his head off at monster jokes. What kind of horse does he ride?
A night mare.

A ghost and a witch with a broom
And a ghoul and a bat in a room
    Stayed up very late
    So that they could debate
About who should be frightened of whom!

In spite of their spooky, kooky, and pukey, icky, sticky, and sicky, and hairy, scary, and extra-ordinary appearance, monsters can be very funny:

Why did the monster eat a light bulb?
    She wanted a light snack. It really brightened her smile and made her eyes light up.

What's yellow on the outside and red, orange, blue, green, brown, and black on the inside?
    A school bus carrying little monsters.

What's the favorite brand of toothpaste for little devils?

Imp-U-Dent.

GIRL: "What's big, yellow, prickly, and has three eyes?"

DAD: "I don't know. What?"

GIRL: "I don't know either, but it's crawling up your leg!"

Where do you find monster snails?

On the end of monsters' fingers.

An upside down monster?
How can you tell?
Its nose will run,
And its feet will smell!

How do you keep an ugly monster in suspense?

I'll tell you tomorrow!

Where can you see a hideous monster?
Look in the mirror!

For your gratification, edification, and trepidation, here's a coven of monsterpieces I've conjured up:

'TWAS HALLOWEEN NIGHT

(Thanks to Clement Clark Moore, who
wrote "The Night Before Christmas.")

'Twas Halloween night,
And all through the house,
All the creatures were stirring
And eating a mouse.

The monsters had gathered
To plan and prepare
For all trick-or-treaters
They wanted to scare.

Each creature stepped forth
And performed energetically
Their Halloween act
And did so alphabetically.

The **Abominable Snowman**,
Known as a Yeti,
Celebrated the night
By tossing confetti.

The **Bats** had a blast,
And they left us aghast!
Through the flap in the bat door
They flew out so fast.

A **Cyclops** awoke,
Afflicted with pink eye.
In a bad-tempered mood,
He gave us the stink eye.

Count Dracula rose,
As he does at night often.
And the whole house was racked
By his terrible coffin.

Frankenstein sat bolt upright
In his 'lectric chair.
"So re-volt-ing! I'm shocked!"
He screamed in despair.

The **Ghosts** were all moaning.
Their voices were heated.
They started their meeting
With "Let's all be sheeted."

A five-legged **Ghoul**
Only mummy could love
Wore polka-dot trousers
That fit like a glove.

Godzilla told jokes.
Please don't think me a louse.
He wasn't that funny,
But he brought down the house.

King-Kong climbed the walls
And chanted some voodoo.
All over the halls,
Monkey see, monkey doo doo.

The long **Loch Ness Monster**,
Her eyes rather bleary,
Decided to go
For a swim in Lake Eerie.

A chummy old **Mummy**
Was no crummy dummy.
She dumped treats yummy, gummy
Into her scummy tummy.

A **Skeleton** offered
A toast quite upbeat,
Raised a mug of formaldehyde:
"Bone appétit!"

A Howl-o-ween **Werewolf**
Ate garlic that night.
All agreed that his breath
Was much worse than his bite.

Into the room
Crept a **Witch** quite inept.
She had just cleaned her house,
And the hag overswept.

All the monsters exclaimed,
As they lurched out of sight,
"Happy Haunting to all —
And to all a good fright!"

DON'T YOU DARE

Don't ever play ping-pong with King-Kong.
Don't ever take blood tests with Dracula.
Don't you dare give a wedgie to Frankenstein.
Your ending will be quite spectaculah!

Don't you dare snap a towel at Godzilla.
Such a prank would be foolishly rude.
Don't you dare floss the teeth of a werewolf.
You are liable to end up as food!

Don't you dare give a hotfoot to Bigfoot.
Don't point a stake at a vampire.
Don't you dare roast marshmallows with
    dragons.
You'll find you are playing with fire!

Don't you steal witches' brooms for spring-
    cleaning.
Don't ever try scaring a ghost.
Don't ever eat breakfast with zombies.
You'll certainly end up on toast!

THE WITCHES' CAULDRON

Double, double, toil and trouble,
Fire burn and cauldron bubble.
Eye of Cyclops, werewolf's claw,
Skeleton's teeth, and King-Kong's paw,
Horseman's head and Hulk's green thumb:
Marinate in ghoul drool scum.
Dragon scales and zombie's ears:
Add a vial of ghostly tears.
Mummy's rags and wing of bat,
Tail of warty witch's cat,
Vampire's fang and Bigfoot's fur:
Give the yucky mix a stir!

I will eat it all with glee,
If it has no broccoli!
I'll swallow all, with happy shouts,
As long as there's no Brussels sprouts!

GOING OUT
ON A LIMERICK

Let us celebrate the limerick, a highly disciplined exercise in light verse that is the most popular fixed poetic form indigenous to the English language. While other basic forms of poetry, such as the sonnet and ode, are borrowed from other countries, the limerick is an original English creation and the most quoted of all verse forms in our language.

> The limerick packs laughs anatomical
> Into space that is quite economical.
> But the good ones I've seen
> So seldom are clean,
> And the clean ones so seldom are comical.
> *-Vivyan Holland*

Despite the opinion expressed in Holland's limerick about limericks, even the clean ones can be comical. Within the brief compass of five lines, the ditty can tell an engaging story or make a humorous statement compactly and cleverly. For some ungodly reason, I love writing limericks about funny monsters:

Tonight, when the last light is gone
And you're sleepy and yawned your last yawn,
    Ghosts and ghouls will come out
    Witches, bats — but don't pout.
All those monsters will leave before dawn.

The **Abominable Snowman** is sweet.
Other monsters he knows how to treat.
    He gave Sasquatch one shoe,
    E width, size twenty-two,
'Cause Sasquatch is Bigfoot, not Bigfeet!

On a blind date, two **Cyclopes** said, "Hi!"
"You're the ONE EYE adore," they did sigh.
    Now they're married for years,
    And the secret appears
To be that they see eye to eye!

You're a woman from East Transylvania
Dating **Dracula**, with his weird mania.
    He asks you each night
    To go out for a bite —
An experience certain to drain ya!

A **dragon** with fiery plume
Crashed a wedding and smashed up the room.
Ate every hors d'oeuvre.
Crushed the cake. What a nerve!
Then toasted the bride and the groom!

Those **ghosts** — Hip, Hooray! Hallelujah!
If you're famous, they're bound to pursue ya.
But here's advice sage:
If you sing on their stage,
The audience surely will boo ya!

Titanic, gigantic **Godzilla**
Stomped on Tokyo, then on Manila.
Then sank a flotilla,
Then fought a gorilla,
And wasn't ashamed one scintilla!

The Hulk wasn't very compliant.
He was mad and annoyed and defiant.
 But he happened to pass
 Anger management class —
And turned into the Jolly Green Giant!

The Invisible Man came to dine.
He sat right to my left, which was fine.
 But his rumblings abdominal
 Were simply phenomenal —
And everyone thought they were mine!

We go ape over **King-Kong**. He's grand.
Biggest monarch in all of the land.
 You might think he's scary,
 But he's tall, dark, and hairy,
And has girls in the palm of his hand!

A monster that took many dips
In **Loch Ness** grew so wide in the hips.
    It was her seafood diet:
    She would see food, then try it.
She especially liked fish and ships!

A talented **mummy** from Ammon
Said, "I make my dad proud and my mom, and
    Though a young whippersnapper,
    I'm the world's greatest wrapper.
I play trumpet, and I Toot Uncommon!"

A bell ringer named **Quasimodo**
Became friends with a hobbit named Frodo.
    "Your back, it's a blob! It
      Is gross!" said the hobbit.
Now that's how to act like a dodo!

An old Roman **skeleton**, Nero,
Is anything but a great hero.
    Some folks think he's shoddy —
      A gutless no body —
With a body mass index of zero!

A well-mannered **vampire** from Wheeling
Was endowed with such delicate feeling.
    When he read on the door,
      "Don't spit on the floor,"
He flew up and spat on the ceiling!

This limerick isn't a stretch.
It's about an unfortunate wretch.
    A **werewolf** pursued him.
    How did he elude him?
He threw it a stick and yelled, "Fetch!"

A **witch** burnt her butt on a candle.
She was angry. It was such a scandal.
    She jumped on her broom
    And zoomed to her doom.
Went too fast, so she flew off the handle!

An innocent fellow named Tim
Met a **zombie** quite horrid and grim.
    Tim patted its head
    Before it had fed.
I wonder what happened to him!

HILARIOUS HALLOWEEN QUOTES

- On Halloween, I ran out of candy and had to give the kids nicotine gum. *-David Letterman*
- I like to get my candy early for Halloween so I have plenty of time to buy more when I eat the first bag. *-Molly Jarrard*
- On Halloween, parents all over America send their kids out looking like me. *-Jimmy Durante*
- Last Halloween was bad for me. I got beat up. I went to a party dressed as a piñata. *-Jim Samuels*
- A Fargo woman will give overweight trick-or-treaters warning letters, not candy. In other news, a woman's house will be egged by fat kids. *-Julius Sharpe*
- I don't get no respect. When I open the door on Halloween, the kids give me candy. *-Rodney Dangerfield*
- I have to be honest. I don't really look forward to Halloween as much as November first.

November first should be named Discount Candy Day. *-Theresa Weaver*

- The other day, I learned that Jehovah's Witnesses do not celebrate Halloween. I guess they don't like strangers going up to their door. *-Bruce Clark*

- When I was twelve, I went as my mother for Halloween. I put on a pair of heels, went door to door, and criticized what everyone else was wearing. *-Robin Bach*

- These masked trick-or-treaters must be confused. They're a day early, came in the back door, passed up the candy, and took the big-screen TV. *-William Ader*

- Be sure to remember when Halloween is. Answering the door when you're three-quarters crocked and finding a pack of midget H-Men, Masters of the Universe, on the front porch can be a scary experience if you're not expecting it. *-P. J. O'Rourke*

- It's that wonderful time of year again when the spider webs I've been too lazy to clean become functional decorations. *-Andy Hardy*

- The worst part about breaking up right before Halloween is now I have to explain at every party why I'm dressed as half of a horse. *-Rob Fee*

- I just asked my husband if he remembers what today is. Scaring men is easy. *-Donna McCoy*

- I don't know that there are real ghosts and goblins, but there are always more trick-or-treaters than neighborhood kids. *-Robert Brault*
- If I'm lazy and I can't come up with a costume, I just wear a slip and write *Freudian* on it. *-Julia Stiles*

- When the box with my Halloween costume arrived, it was empty. I called the company and asked where my Queen Elizabeth costume was. They apologized, said they would ship my costume the next day, and I could keep the Lady Godiva costume I got by mistake. *-Anonymous*

A JUMBLED HALLOWEEN

Unscramble each set of letters to form a Halloween word or words. Examples: DOILYHA = *holiday* and ALLOWNEHE = *Halloween.*

1. SKYOOP
2. MIPPUNK
3. DAYCN
4. MUSSCOTE
5. SHOTSG

6. CHESTIW
7. NOSESTMR
8. DUNEHAT SHEUO
9. KCAJ O'TRANNEL
10. KRICT RO TATER

ANSWERS

1. spooky 2. pumpkin 3. candy 4. costumes 5. ghosts 6. witches 7. monsters 8. haunted house 9. jack-o'-lantern 10. trick or treat

DON'T KNOCK
KNOCK-KNOCKS

Knock, knock.
Who's there?
Wooden shoe.
Wooden shoe who?
Wooden shoe like to hear a bunch of Halloween knock-knock jokes?

Knock, knock.
Who's there?
Boo!
Boo who?
Don't cry. You're about to laugh at some Halloween jokes.

Knock, knock.
Who's there?
Hearsay.
Hearsay who?
Hearsay parade of Halloween knock-knock jokes.

Knock, knock.
Who's there?
Eyesore.
Eyesore who?
Eyesore like knock-knock jokes,

Knock, knock.
Who's there?
Howl.
Howl who?
Howl you be dressed up for Halloween?

Knock, knock.
Who's there?
Phillip.
Phillip who?
Phillip my bag with Halloween candy.

Knock, knock.
Who's there?
Aida.
Aida who?
Aida lot of candy on Halloween.

Knock, knock.
Who's there?
Armageddon.
Armageddon who?
Armageddon out of the way of any monster I meet.

Knock, knock.
Who's there?
Achoo.
Achoo who?
"Achoo on people's necks!" boasted the vampire.

Knock, knock.
Who's there?
Ice cream.
Ice cream who?
Ice cream whenever I see a ghost.

Knock, knock.
Who's there?
Ivan.
Ivan who?
Ivan to drink your blood.

Knock, knock.
Who's there?
Discount.
Discount who?
Discount is named Dracula!

Knock, knock.
Who's there?
Hair comb.
Hair comb who?
Hair comb a pack of werewolves.

Knock, knock.
Who's there?
Decry.
Decry who?
Decry of de werewolf sends shivers up de spine.

Knock, knock.
Who's there?
Wanda.
Wanda who?
Wanda go for a ride on a witch's broomstick?

Knock, knock.
Who's there?
Witch.
Witch who?
Witch way to the haunted house?

Knock, knock.
Who's there?
Witch.
Witch who?
Gesundheit!

Knock, knock.
Who's there?
Zombies.
Zombies who?
Zombies make honey and zombies don't.

Knock, knock.
Who's there?
Amsterdam.
Amsterdam who?
Amsterdam tired of these knock-knock jokes.

Knock, knock.
Who's there?
Consumption.
Consumption who?
Consumption be done to stop these ridiculous knock-knock jokes?

Knock, knock.
Who's there?
Celeste.
Celeste who?
Celeste time I tell you to knock it off!

Knock, knock.
Who's there?
Orange juice.
Orange juice who?
Orange juice glad that this'll be my very last knock-knock joke?

PUNS SPOOKEN HERE

Punnery is the trick of compacting two or more ideas within a single word or expression. It surprises us by flouting the law of nature that pretends that two things cannot occupy the same space at the same time. Punnery is an exercise of the mind in being concise. It challenges us to apply the greatest pressure per square syllable of language.

Punnery is a rewording experience, especially around Halloween:

The spirited Halloween ball was a site for soirees. Hundreds of specters from ghost to ghost traveled to the gala event held in Mali-Boo. The ghostly band played haunting melodies, such as "Ghost Riders in the Sky," and the ghosts boo-gied and danced sheet to sheet.

One of the apparitions was dressed in red and green. He was a Christmas wraith. Another came dressed up in a moth-eaten sheet. He was a holy terror.

A number of the ghosts raised their goblets of boos in ghost toasts to dampen the spirits. As they became increasingly drunk and disorderly, one of the specters observed, "Just like when he was alive working as a bicycle mechanic, the bartender got the spooks too tight."

The *X-Files* staff wished to take a picture of one of the ghosts at the ball. Because the event took place during darkest night, they decided to use flash photography. The ghost agreed to have his picture taken, but the photographer couldn't get the flash to work. The spirit was willing but the flash was weak. As a result, all the *X-Files* staff was able to develop was the Prints of Darkness.

The ghostly children came dressed up in white pillowcases. Little ghosts love playing games like hide and shriek and peek-a-boo! Their favorite amusement park rides are the scare-ousel and the roller ghoster.

Small ghosts often attend dayscare centers, located on dead ends. Little boy ghosts assemble toy ghost towns. Little girl ghosts play with their haunted dollhouses.

Their trans parents advise them,

- "Remember to boo-ckle your sheet belt."
- "Spook only when spooken to."
- "Remember to say, 'How do you boo, sir or madam?'"

If the ghostlets don't obey, their trans parents make them ghost stand in a corner in the living room.

Now that the ghost is clear, it's time for some ghostly riddles. You have more than a ghost of a chance of avoiding boo-boos and coming up with right answers.

Why are ghosts bad liars?
You can see right through them.

What do you call a chicken that haunts your house?
A poultrygeist.

Why was the ghost surprised when his girlfriend showed up for their date early?
He didn't ex-specter until midnight.

What happened when the little ghost fell and scraped his knee?

He got a boo-boo.

Where do Native American ghosts hang out?

At the Happy Haunting Grounds.

What do you get when you cross Bambi with a ghost?

Bamboo.

What do you get if you cross fake chocolate with the ghost of a reindeer?

Carob–boo.

What do you call a ghost who haunts small hotels?

An inn specter.

What do you use to get into a haunted house?

A spook key.

Why did the game warden arrest the ghost?

He didn't have a haunting license.

What do you call a ghost that sits in the picture window of a haunted house?

A window shade.

Why does an elevator make ghosts happy?

Because it lifts the spirits.

What do you call the ghosts of dead turkeys?
Gobblins.

Where do ghosts go shopping?
In boo-tiques.

What happens when a ghost haunts a theater?
The actors get stage fright.

How does an exorcist keep in shape?
She rides an exorcycle.

What happens when you fire your exorcist?
You get ex-spelled and repossessed.

What do spooks call their navy?
The Ghost Guard.

FUNNY BONES

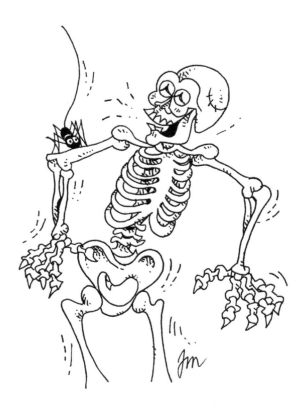

A lot of people make no bones about taunting skeletons. "Get a life, lazybones!" they sneer.

"You're a bonehead! You're a bag of bones! You're totally heartless and gutless! You're a no body!"

But let's face facts. We are all skeletons wearing skin. So if you want to become a skeleton, go out into the woods at midnight and get so frightened that you jump out of your skin! Like human beings, skeletons have a wide range of emotions: They can be humerus, they can be sternum, and they can be hot under the collarbone.

Skeletons usually don't go to parties. Their Facebook pictures are X-rays, which other creatures don't find attractive. So they don't have any body to dance with, they don't have the stomach for it, and their hearts aren't in it.

When a skeleton does attend a party, she hopes to have a bone-rattling good time and engage in some skull-duggery. So she starts by saying to the bartender, "I can't hold my liquor, so I'll have a pop and a mop!" The other guests try to use her as a coat rack, and the musicians try to play her like a xylophone. But the skeleton stays calm because nothing gets under her skin, and it's no skin off her nose. She just lifts her glass and says, "Bone appétit."

Skeleton families are quite up-to-date. Long ago, they gave up their landline skelephones for new cell bones. The families go out to eat at cadaver-terias, where they enjoy devouring spare ribs, T-bone steaks, and skullions served on bone china. For recreation, they go skulling on the Skull Kill River.

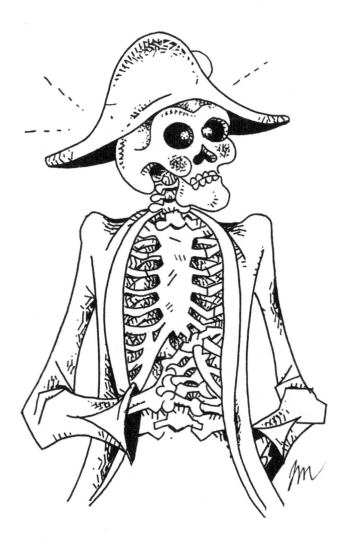

At home, the children take lessons on the trom-bone, and the families enjoy reading history books about Napoleon Bone-apart and Lady Cadaver. Their favorite TV and movie characters are Bones on *Star Trek* and Sherlock Bones, as played by Basil

Wrath-Bone. Outside their homes they hang pirate flags with skulls and crossbones.

Mama and papa skeletons offer their children suggestions for a better life:

- "Drink at least ten glasses of milk a day. It's good for your bones."
- "Never play with werewolves. They're just after your bones!"
- "In winter, wear a hat and a warm coat, or you'll be a numbskull and the cold will go right through you."
- "Listen to what I tell you! I worked my fingers to the bone for you!"

Are you ready to bone up on skeletons?

Knock, knock.
Who's there?
Defeat.
Defeat who?
Defeat bones connected to de ankle bones.

Now, have a rattling good time with a bone-us of some bone-chilling, spine-tingling, rib-tickling riddles:

What do you use to get into a locked cemetery?
A skeleton key.

Why did the skeleton cross the road?
To get to the body shop.

What's the scariest job in the world?
  The graveyard shift with a skeleton crew.

How did the skeleton know it was going to rain?
  She could feel it in her bones.

How did the skeleton woo his girlfriend on Valentine's Day?
  He said, "I love every bone in your body!" and gave her bone-bones in a heart-shaped box.

Why can't skeletons play music in church?
  They don't have any organs.

Why are skeletons always bone dry?

No sweat.

What do you call a skeleton who's always telling lies?

A bony phony.

What do skeletons do when the electricity goes out in their homes?

They plug their appliances into their eye sockets.

What did the skeleton say at the start of her magic act?

"Abra-cadaver!"

Why did the skeleton princess remain unmarried her whole life?

Because her father felt that no male skeleton cadaver.

Why was the werewolf angry at the skeleton?

He had many bones to pick with him.

What did the werewolf say to the skeleton?

"It's been nice gnawing you."

What do you call a skeleton who doesn't have all her fingers on one hand?

Normal. Fingers are usually divided equally between its two hands.

When does a skeleton laugh?
When something tickles her funny bone.

As skeletons say to their friends who are going on cruises, "Bone voyage!"

THE WITCHING HOUR

Halloween is the time for witchful thinking.

Witches are flying sorcerers. On October 31, they look at their witch watches, hop on their brooms, and sweep through the Halloween skies. When they're in a rush, they get on the stick, the broomstick, that is. They prefer to ride brooms because vacuum cleaners are too heavy, and the electric cord isn't long enough.

If their broom happens to break, they witch-hike, or they call broom service. Sometimes they take scareplanes and fly to Witch-ita, Kansas; Witchmond, Virginia; and Green Witch, Connecticut.

Actually, I tried to join a coven myself, but the doors warlocked. That's because there had just been a panty raid on the coven. It was an embarrassment of witches.

Witches' faces look like a million dollars, all green and wrinkly. Witches actually hire out their faces as a cure for hiccups. Their faces are so ugly that they turn Medusa to stone. They're so ugly that their hair hangs down to their waist, from under their armpits. Their husbands take them to work because they don't want to kiss them goodbye. Witches think they're funny because every time they look in the mirror, it cracks up.

Witches are so ugly that when a witch baby is born, the doctor slaps her mother and the birth certificate is a letter of apology. But witches take good care of their little baby broomers. They feed them a lot of healthy magic formula in the morning and sing lullabies to help the little tykes go to sweep. They serve them Lucky Charms and Rice Kreepies, which go "Snap! Cackle! and Pop!"

Instead of using cauldrons, little witches stir strange ingredients in soup bowls and fly around on whisk brooms.

Groan-up witches offer their kids a frothy brew of wisdom and counsel:

- "Study hard for your hexaminations, especially in spelling. If you don't, you could get ex-spelled."
- "If you're in a bathroom stall next to one occupied by a mummy, do not use her bandages as toilet paper!"
- "Don't ask for the keys to the broom more than once a week."

Many witches end up on radio. They have the perfect face for it. If they want to appear on television, they make themselves attractive and bewitching by dieting with Weight Witches, driving their Ford Hocus Pocus to a scare dresser at the ugly parlor and applying scare spray and mass-scare-a. They often become weather witches because they're so good at forecasting. The more charming ones end up appearing on *Lifestyles of the Witch and Famous.*

One witch became a movie star. She teamed with a werewolf in the famous film *Ugly and the Beast*, directed by Stephen Spellberg. Another witch had the face of a beauty queen, but she had to give it back.

Witches love to be entertained. Their favorite music is hagtime, and their favorite songs are "It's Not Easy Being Green," "We're Off to See the Wizard," and "Help Me, Wand-a."

Their favorite movie series is *Star Warlocks*, and their favorite movie characters are The Wicked Witch of the West and Warlock Holmes.

Their favorite fairy tale is *Sleeping Ugly,* and their favorite cartoon characters are Broom Hilda, The Wizard of Id, and Wand-a Woman.

Teen witches often attend Poison Ivy League universities. They especially enjoy studying spelling and black-arts and witchcrafts, but when the witch said, "Duble, duble, toyl and truble," nothing happened. She was a hopeless speller.

Witches often keep pets, such as bats and snakes. One witch contracted a skin disease from her pet and went from bat to warts. Another attached her pet snake to the front window of her automobile and used it as a witch shield viper.

Witches love to play baseball. One team of witches had a one-run lead going into the last inning. They wanted to increase their advantage, but their bats flew away. Fortunately, their star pitcher finally arrived for the ninth inning and, applying her pitch-craft, struck out the other side. That's how a witch in time saved nine.

One Halloween, a little witch went trick-or-treating and collecting goodies in her hag bag. For her costume, she draped herself with several strings of blinking Christmas tree bulbs. She was a lights witch.

Here's a bubbly cauldron of black magic riddles about witches.

What is the witches' motto?
"I came. I saw. I conjured."

What contests do witches always win?
Ugly pageants.

What do you call an insect witch?
A coven-ant.

What do witches call their garages?
Broom closets.

What do Australian witches ride on?
Broomerangs.

What did the witch name her cooking pot?
It was called Ron.

Why are witches like candles?
They're both wick-ed.

Why do witches use pencil sharpeners?
To keep their hats pointy and their broomsticks cutting edge.

Why don't witches wear flat hats?
Because there's no point to them, so the witches look like dorks.

Did you hear about the witch who was born with an upside-down nose?
Every time she sneezed, her hat blew off.

Did you hear about the witch who gave up fortune telling?
She couldn't see any future in it.

Did you hear about the witch who sprinkles poison on people's Corn Flakes?
She's a cereal killer.

How do you make a witch scratch?
Take away her "w."

Why did the twin witches wear name tags?
So that everyone could tell which witch was which.

Who flies on a broom and carries a medicine bag?
A witch doctor.

What do you get when you cross a witch with an insect?
A spelling bee.

What do you get when you cross a witch with Mickey Mouse?
Disney spells.

What do you get when you cross a mute owl with a witch?

A creature that doesn't give a hoot about being ugly.

What's the difference between a deer and a small witch?

One is a hunted stag, and the other is a stunted hag.

What's the difference between a store where humans shop and one where witches shop?

One is a Wal-Mart, and the other is a Mall-Wart.

What do you call a nervous witch?

A twitch.

What do you call two witches who live together?

Broommates.

What do you call a witch who lives on the beach?

A sand witch.

Why do witches get good bargains?

Because they like to hag-gle.

Why did the witch send her broom to the dry cleaner?

She wanted a clean sweep.

If you meet a witch in a bog,
On a rock, or a stump, or a log,
   It really is better
   That you don't upset her.
She might turn you into a frog!

Once upon a time in England, a very mean witch was terrorizing the local population, who finally went to the resident wizard to see what could be done about her.

The wizard gave them a potion that would turn the witch into a statue. The townspeople managed to put the potion in the witch's food. When she found out about this, she turned green with rage, but it was too late, and the potion worked as expected.

The jubilant population had a big celebration and parade and placed the petrified witch in a park as a public example. Pretty soon, people discovered that the witch had been frozen in a position that made her a perfect sundial, and they started using her to tell the time of day. The custom grew and, that's why people often refer to Mean Green Witch Time.

What has six legs and flies?

A witch and her cat on a broom stick.

When is it bad luck for a black cat to cross your path?

When you're a mouse.

What happened when the witch's pet fell off her broomstick?

It was a cat-astrophe.

How many witches does it take to change a light bulb?

Just one — and she changes it into a black cat.

What do you get when you cross a witch's cat with a canary?

A peeping tom.

What do you get when you cross a witch's cat with a lemon?

A sour puss.

Witches often have black cats as their pets. In the following challenge, come up with words that begin with *black* and *cat*. The first ten begin with *black*. Example: This *black* is a witch's companion: *black cat.*

1. This *black* is a slate in a classroom.
2. This *black* is the highest rank in judo or karate.
3. This *black* is a coerced payment.
4. This *black* is a small volume of telephone numbers.
5. This *black* is a metalworker.

6. This *black* is a weapon.
7. This *black* is to be excluded.
8. This *black* is an astronomical object of incredible gravity.
9. This *black* is a villain.
10. This *black* is dark comedy.

The next ten words all begin with the letters *c-a-t*. Example: This cat hurls rocks at castles: *catapult*.

11. This *cat* is a disaster.
12. This *cat* is a descriptive booklet.
13. This *cat* is a huge waterfall.
14. This *cat* tastes good on a hamburger.
15. This *cat* is classified.

16. This *cat* is cryptically buried underground.
17. This *cat* speeds a chemical reaction.
18. This *cat* chirps.
19. This *cat* swims.
20. This *cat* hopes one day to flutter by.

ANSWERS

1. blackboard 2. black belt 3. blackmail 4. little black book 5. blacksmith 6. blackjack 7. blackballed / blacklisted 8. black hole 9. blackguard 10. black humor

11. catastrophe 12. catalog 13. cataract 14. catsup 15. category 16. catacomb 17. catalyst 18. catbird 19. catfish 20. caterpillar

WORD PREY IN A JUGULAR VEIN

Three vampires went into a bar. A buxom barmaid came over to take their orders. The vampires flirted with her by telling her how much they liked her blood type. But she rebuffed them with the reply "O negative" and asked, "And what would you gentlemen like tonight?"

The first vampire said, "I'll have a mug of blood."

The second vampire said, "I'll have a mug of blood."

The third vampire said, "I'll have a glass of plasma."

The barmaid called out to the bartender, "Two bloods and a blood light!"

Then they all toasted each other with "This blood's for you!"

Vampires love to drink blood because they find it thicker than water. I know a vampire who worked as a night watchman at a blood bank. He took too many coffin breaks, and they caught him making unauthorized withdrawals. He was fired for drinking on the job.

Long ago vampires sailed to the United States in blood vessels — many of them working as Stokers — and set up their own terror-tories. Some settled in the Vampire State, and others went west and became batboys for the Colorado Rockies Horror Picture Show. Some went on to college and earned a place in Phi Batta Cape-a. Others perfected their skills at sucking blood by working for the IRS.

Vampires from all over the world gather each fall deep in the forests of Transylvania to renew their commitment to their calling. At midnight, they stand at attention and swear allegiance to the Draculation of Vein Dependence.

The most famous of all vampires is, of course, Count Dracula, the notorious neck-romancer. He lives at the dead end of a psycho path, in a petrified dreadwood forest in Tombstone, Arizona. In his two-car garage you will find a Batmobile and a Bloodmobile.

When he was a batboy, he played bat's cradle and battycake and learned the alphabat so that he could read books like *The Bat in the Hat.* Now the Count loves to sing "You're So Vein," "Bloody Mary is the Girl for Me," and "Fangs for the Mammaries." He reads *The Rise and Fall of the Roman Vampire* and, because it has great circulation, *Bleeder's Digest.*

Dracula once fell in love at first fright with the vampiress necks door. She was six feet tall, and Dracula loves to suck up to women. But he's remained a bat-chelor his whole life because anytime he courts another vampire, they end up at each other's throats, screaming, "You suck!" and "Bite me!"

Any mortal woman to whom Dracula is attracted soon realizes that life with him will be an unfailingly draining experience, so she's not likely to stick her neck out for him. The Count can be a real pain in the neck, and he can get under your skin. Even if he pays for dinner, he'll still put the bite on you. It's hard to get a good day's sleep with him because of his terrible coffin.

Moreover, Dracula isn't a very attractive fellow, in large part because he can't see himself in the bat room mirror so is unable to comb his hair or tie his tie. Dracula is afflicted with bat breath and the disease he fears most — tooth decay. The fiend once went to the dentist to correct his bite, but he still ended up with false teeth, which for him are new-fang-led devices that, like Dracula himself, come out at night.

Dracula finds his victims in any neck of the woods. Whenever the police come after him, the count simply explains that he is a law-a-biting citizen.

The vampire starts all his letters with "Tomb it may concern." He loves the deep plots and grave setting of a cemetery, especially when the temperature rises above ninety degrees. Dracula often sighs, "There's nothing like a cold bier on a hot day."

Mummies and batties tell their vampire kids at an early age,

- "Stop opening the can of tomato juice with your fangs."
- "Stop sucking all the jelly out of the donuts."
- "Drink your soup before it clots."
- "Always bite the hand that feeds you."
- "Always be scareful. Don't ever bite your lip."
- "Do your homework and you'll score high on blood tests."
- "Whatever else you do, never run with a wooden stake in your hands."
- "Don't cry over spilled blood."
- "Remember to apply #90 sun block every day."

- "Never enter the sweepstakes or play high-stakes poker."

- "Don't act like a spoiled bat!"

Even with this sound advice, vampire children can become spoiled bats and drive their parents batty.

Here are some riddles that you can really sink your teeth into.

What is a little vampire's favorite Christmas song?

"I saw mummy hissing Santa's claws."

What did the vampire do when he saw a funeral procession?

He took a turn for the hearse.

What do vampires take for a sore throat?

Coffin drops.

Did you hear about the vampire's arithmetic homework assignment?

It was a blood count.

Did you hear about the vampire in jail?

He was in a blood cell.

Did you hear about the Native American vampire?
He was a full-blooded Indian.

Who went to the vampires' family reunion?
All of the blood relations.

Who sends letters to Dracula?
His fang club.

Why did the vampire go to the orthodontist?
To improve his bite.

How can you spot a vampire jockey?
He always wins by a neck.

Why did the vampire join the police force?
So he could learn the correct way to get a stakeout.

VAMPIRE TEACHER: How do you spell *coffin?*
LITTLE DRACULA: K-A-U-G-H-E-N.
VAMPIRE TEACHER: That's the worst *coffin* spell I have ever heard.

How did the vampire killer dispatch Dracula?
Painstakingly.

Did you hear about the unsuccessful vampire hunter?
He tried to kill a vampire by driving a pork chop through its heart because steaks were too expensive.

Where do they cremate seductive women?
On vamp pyres.

Where does Count Dracula usually eat his lunch?
At the casketeria, where he stops in for a quick bite.

What is Dracula's favorite animal?
The giraffe. There's so much neck to suck on.

What did Dracula say to his elderly apprentice?
"We could use some new blood around here."

Why are there so many vampires in Hollywood?
Somebody has to play the bit parts.

How did the race between two vampires end?
They finished neck and neck.

How many vampires does it take to change a light bulb?
None. Vampires prefer the dark.

Vampires don't like to be crossed, but they often are, as the following creepy hybrids will show:

What do you get if you cross a vampire and a vegetarian?
Something that tries to get blood from a turnip.

What do you get when you cross Dracula with a snowman?
Frostbite.

What do you get when you cross Dracula with a dog?
Something whose bite is worse than its bark.

What do you get when you cross Dracula with Long John Silver?

A vampirate.

What do you get when you cross Dracula and a fish?

Cape Cod.

What do you get when you cross Dracula and a duck?

Count Drakeula.

What do you get when you cross Dracula with a large antlered animal?

Vamoose!

Now it's time to say goodbye to Dracula and his batty friends. "So long, suckers!"

A STITCH IN STEIN

A loony doctor's weird intention
Made a freak of dark dimension.
The mention of his scarred invention
Created tension, deep dissension.

Frankenstein got struck by lightning,
Terror in the village heightening.
Throats of villagers were tightening.
Nothing brightening, all so frightening.

Stitched-up brutes are so re-volt-ing,
Terrifying stress resulting.
They generate shock that is so jolting
That panicked villagers are bolt-ing.

Doctor Victor Frankenstein was the world's first body builder. He created his monster because he liked to make new friends. For his groundbreaking work, he was awarded a Nobel Pieces Prize.

Frankenstein employed a band of headhunters to gather body parts to make his monster. They chopped up corpses and placed the pieces in a box with the label "Some Assembly Required." The doctor had his work cut out for him.

The mad scientist thought his monster needed a brain like he needed a hole in the head. Frankenstein had half a mind to make his monster with nothing inside his head, but that would have been a no-brainer. Instead, the doctor picked his monster's brain because he liked to change people's minds. It gave the monster a piece of mind.

Using a dead bolt, he made sure that his creation had a good head on his shoulders. The result: Dr. Frankenstein put together a Lost Neck Monster.

Despite his evil reputation, Doctor Frankenstein actually had a good sense of humor and always kept his monster in stitches. When the monster asked the doctor if he could sew himself up, the mad scientist replied, "Sure, suture self!" That made the monster knit his brow, but like two curtains, he ultimately pulled himself together.

When Frankenstein's monster was struck by lightning, it was like a bolt from the blue. The fiend screamed, "Aw shocks! I get such a charge out this! It's just watt I need! I'm a live wire!" When the brute rose from the table and spat on the ground, the proud doctor exclaimed, "It's saliva! It's saliva!" That was an electrifying moment — when the monster met his maker.

The monster had a tough time in high school. His classmates teased him about his gray complexion and dorky wardrobe. They told him that he looked like death warmed over.

Later, whenever the monster sent his picture to a Lonely Hearts Club, they wrote back and said, sorry, nobody here is that lonely! Whenever a girl ghoul was attracted to him, he developed a crush on her and gave her a choker. When she became his main squeeze, that was the end of her. That's why they called him a lady-killer.

Frankenstein's monster had his heart in the right place. In fact, he once had a ghoul friend to take out for a frank 'n' stein. He just couldn't resistor. He told her, "Frank-ly, I love you a whole watt! You've stolen my heart! Please be my valenstein!"

He also dated a lady scarecrow but went from rags to witches. She was his last straw. In general, the monster's romantic relationships didn't last very long because the nut screwed around and then bolted.

When Doctor Frankenstein ran out of corpses, he had an out-of-bodies experience. So he found a new job at a body shop as parts manager.

Frankenstein's monster's favorite shock-and-soul singer was Carmen Electricity, and his favorite songs were "Put on a Happy Face" and "I Fall to Pieces." He always stood bolt upright when "The Scar Strangled Banner" was played, and his favorite musical comedy by far was *Little Shock of Horrors*. His favorite athlete was Usain Bolt, and his favorite NFL team the Los Angeles Chargers.

Frankenstein's monster sat on a wall.
Frankenstein's monster had a great fall.
All the king's horses and all the king's men
Can't sew the body parts together again!

Sensitive fellow that Frankenstein's monster was, he developed an identity crisis. Whenever someone asked him, "Who do you think you are?" he would answer, "Tom, Dick, Harry, Rodney, George, Bruce, José…" The monster kept hoping that he had a mummy and deady, but he was never able to dig them up.

He went to a psychiatrist to see if his head was screwed on right. "I'm at loose ends. I'm coming apart at the seams."

He complained to the psychiatrist, "I seem to be going around in circles."

Said the doctor, "That's because somebody has nailed your foot to the floor!"

Frankenstein's monster had five hundred followers. Unfortunately, they all carried torches and pitchforks. When the villagers chased the monster, he shrieked at them, "Do you want a piece of me?" When the villagers buried the big guy, his tombstone read, "Rest in Pieces."

I hope the riddles that follow will keep you in stitches:

What did young Victor Frankenstein say to his English teacher when she asked him for his book report?

"My homework ate the dog!"

What mad scientist played the most practical jokes?

Prankenstein.

What do you call a brilliant scientist?

Frank Einstein.

What scientist flies his kite in a thunderstorm?

Benjamin Frankenstein.

What's big and grotesque and goes, "Oink, oink"?
Frankenswine.

What does Doctor Frankenstein use to go fishing for electric eels?
A lightning rod.

What gifts did the three wise men bring to the manger?
Gold, Frankenstein, and myrrh.

Why does Frankenstein's monster hate flying?
Because every time he goes to an airport, his bolts set off an alarm.

How do you keep the monster from biting his nails?
Give him some nuts, bolts, and screws instead.

How did the monster eat his lunch?
He bolted it down.

How did the monster win the election?
He got all the volts.

If Al Franken and Ben Stein ran for president and vice president, what would their posters say?
"Vote for Franken-Stein."

Why can't the monster finish running a marathon?
He always gets a stitch in his side.

I HAVE A HUNCH

Quasimodo wasn't the quarterback or the half-back or even the fullback of Notre Dame. Rather, he was the hunchback of Notre Dame, in the novel of that title by French writer Victor Hugo.

Having grown too old to scale the tower and ring the bells, Quasimodo ran an ad in the local newspaper for a replacement. An armless man appeared at the old man's door. The old ring-master asked him, "Are you here for the job of bell ringer?"

"Yes, I am."

"But how can you ring the bell when you have no arms?"

"That's easy. I may lack arms, but I've got an extremely tough skull. I simply run at the bell and strike it with my forehead. The tone produced is absolutely exquisite.

Finding the man disarming, Quasimodo hired him as bell ringer.

The man ascended the spiral staircase, climbed into the bell tower, ran at the bell, and struck it with his forehead, indeed making a lovely clang. Alas, though, the bell swung back pendularly, smashed into the poor chap, and knocked him out of the tower. He flew through the air and splatted on the cobblestones far below.

When the police arrived at the scene, an officer asked, "Mr. Quasimodo, do you know this man?"

"Yes, I do," answered Quasi. "He was an employee of mine."

"For our records, please give us his name."

91

Quasimodo furrowed his brow. "I don't know his name, but his face rings a bell!"

Shortly thereafter, Quasimodo placed a second ad in the paper asking for new bell-ringing applicants. A second gentleman appeared who looked exactly like the first, including the state of armlessness.

Quasimodo asked the new man, "Are you applying for the job of bell ringer?

"Yes, I am," replied the second man.

"Then I have two questions for you. First, am I wrong or do you look exactly like another fellow who was recently in my employ but who jumped to a conclusion? In fact, he could be your doppelgonger."

"That man was my older brother," replied the applicant. "Indeed, many people have remarked that he and I looked like twins."

"You look so much like him," Quasimodo went on, "that you too lack arms. How do you propose to ring the bell?"

"Easy. Like my brother, I have an exceedingly tough forehead, which I use to ring the bell. But I am more agile than my brother, and I have learned to get out of the way of the bell's backswing."

"Fine," sighed Quasimodo with relief. "You may start work immediately."

The second gentleman mounted the spiral staircase, climbed up to the tower, and ran headlong into the bell, producing as exquisite a tone as had his brother. As the bell swayed back toward him, he deftly stepped aside and avoided getting clobbered by the return swing.

Alas, though, three nights later, the new bell ringer got stinking drunk. He staggered up the spiral staircase, lurched toward the bell, and struck a glancing blow with his forehead. As he stood there swaying, the bell swung back and knocked him out of the tower. He flew through the air and, like his brother, splatted on the cobblestones below.

Again the police arrived. "Do you know *this* man, Mr. Quasimodo?"

"Yes, he too was an employee of mine," sighed the hunchback.

"May we have his name, please?"

"I don't know his name either, but he's a dead ringer for his brother!"

A HALLOWEEN SICK-TIONARY

Bat: A fly-by-night mammal with lots of hangups.

Boogieman: A monster who loves to dance disco.

Coffin: What you are doing when you get a piece of popcorn stuck in your throat.

Cyclops: A monster with 20 vision who wears a monocle and gives you the evil eye.

Demon: A ghoul's buddy, as in "Demons are a ghoul's best friend."

Dracula: An infamous bloodsucker and neckrophiliac.

Frankenstein's Monster: Old Zipperneck.

Full Moon: What your repairman reveals when he bends over to fix your sink.

Ghost: A spooksperson.

Ghoul: A monster who is always dead on her feet, rotten to the core, and eats the brains out of the center of Halloween pumpkins.

Goblin: How you eat the candy bars from your Halloween treat bag.

The Headless Horseman: A fellow who wanted to get a head in life.

The Hulk: The Unjolly Green Giant.

Invisible Man: What a guy becomes when there's housework to be done.

Jack-O'-Lantern: An Irish Pumpkin.

Jack the Ripper: What Jack does to his lottery tickets after losing each week.

King-Kong: A gargantuan gorilla to go ape over. Do not monkey around with this monkey.

Mummy: A monster who's all wrapped up in herself.

Pumpkin Patch: What a pumpkin pirate wears over one eye.

Quasimodo: A Hump-ty Dumpty fellow.

Skeleton: What is left after the outsides have been taken off and insides have been taken out.

Spider: An insect with its own website.

Vampire: One who believes that there's a sucker born every minute.

Vampire Bat: What Dracula hits a baseball with.

Werewolf: A Howl-o-ween monster who has to comb his face.

Witch: A frequent flyer who gets on the stick.

Zombie: What you look like before that first cup of morning coffee.

ACKNOWLEDGMENTS

I am grateful for permission to adapt in *A Treasury of Halloween Humor* versions of some items that have appeared in my Gibbs Smith and Marion Street Press books.

AUTHOR BIOGRAPHY

Richard Lederer is the author of more than fifty books about language, history, and humor, including his best-selling *Anguished English* series and his current books, *The Joy of Names* and *A Treasury of Christmas Humor*. He is a founding co-host of *A Way With Words*, broadcast on Public Radio.

Dr. Lederer's syndicated column, *Lederer on Language*, appears in newspapers and magazines throughout the United States. He has been named International Punster of the Year and Toastmasters International's Golden Gavel winner.

He lives in San Diego with his wife, Simone van Egeren.

richardhlederer@gmail.com / verbivore.com

PORTRAIT OF
THE ARTIST

Jim McLean has enjoyed a thirty-three year career as a professor of art. He has exhibited internationally and has works in a number of museums, universities, and private collections. Since his retirement in 1994, Jim's interest in cartooning led him to a productive collaboration with Richard Lederer, for whom he has illustrated fifteen books.

mcle231@bellsouth.net

Made in the USA
Middletown, DE
19 September 2022

10153282R00066